The Really Bad Thing
About Free Will

Also by Martin Zender

*How to Quit Church
Without Quitting God*

*Martin Zender's Guide to
Intelligent Prayer*

Martin Zender Goes To Hell

Flawed by Design

*How to be Free From Sin
While Smoking a Cigarette*

The First Idiot in Heaven

THE REALLY BAD THING ABOUT
FREE WILL

A CRITICAL LOOK AT THE
SALVATION BY WILLPOWER
DOCTRINE

m a r t i n   z e n d e r

STARKE & HARTMANN

The Really Bad Thing About Free Will

© 2006 by Martin Zender

Published by Starke & Hartmann
P.O. Box 6473
Canton, OH   44706
www.starkehartmann.com
1-866-866-BOOK

Printed in the United States of America

To my Lord and Savior

"For in grace, through faith, are you saved, and this is not out of you; it is God's approach present, not of works, lest anyone should be boasting."

—*the apostle Paul*
Ephesians 2:8-9

I would like to thank my friend Michael B. Telep of North Royalton, Ohio, for portraying an honest and consistent free will person on the cover of this book. I couldn't find the genuine article, so I forced Mike into this contortion. For Mike's sake, I'll call his cover character "Dave." It's the least I can do for not paying Mike for his services.

On the cover, Dave is celebrating his decision to believe in Jesus. It's an honest photo because Dave does deserve the credit. Let's all be honest. If God gave Dave belief, then God would deserve the credit. But God does not give anyone belief. He can't!

Many years ago, God gave each human, including Dave, a free will. God respects this sovereign area of humanity so much that He refuses to invade it. To invade a human's inherent unbelief and just drop faith into his lap would be interference of the highest order.

If God did it for one person, the question would come: "Why not do it for all?" God probably, at one time, considered this. *Good heavens,* thought God. *If I gave belief to all, then all would be saved. Not only that, but the glory and the credit for it would be Mine and not theirs. There would be no personal glory for anybody.* God instinctively knew what a terrible situation this would be for the industry of religion.

And so, when it came down to the most monumental decision in life, God would leave everyone completely alone. He sighed sadly at this decision. But really, it was an inevitable consequence of free will. Oh, God might bend the rules occasionally and impart hope to someone. Occasionally, He might help someone raise a child, or buy the right car, or locate a fuse box in the dark. He might even divert a man headed for trouble toward a righteous path, or take away a mother's tear. But at crunch time—that is, at the all-important hour of decision—it would be every man for himself. No one would ever accuse "The Man Upstairs" of playing favorites.

Dave understands these things. He knows that while God may lead a person to the altar, He will not make him believe. Jesus made it possible for humankind to believe and be saved, but neither He nor God will make a person do it. Thus, Jesus does not save, and neither does God. Well? Is paving the way to salvation the same as salvation itself? Is the sidewalk *to* a house the same as the house? Let's be honest. Jesus only makes it possible for people to save themselves by believing. Praise Jesus for salvation? Not unless you're a hypocrite. Rather, praise Jesus for the possibility of it. Praise Jesus, yes, for the opportunity afforded man to exercise faith. But praise Dave for the salvation itself. Because Dave acted while God left him completely alone to exercise his free will.

The minister at the altar call had said to Dave: "Come forward and be saved!" Why would the minister have said that if Jesus had already saved Dave? Apparently, Jesus had not saved him yet—all that work at the cross, and *still* no salvation. What the minister should have said was, "Come forward and accomplish what Jesus left undone." But have you ever heard a minister who was that honest?

Only Dave could make salvation real for himself, and he did. Dave did it! He managed to accomplish what millions of other people could not, that is, he worked up sufficient faith to satisfy God.

Praise Dave.

Jesus or willpower: Behind the mask

The apostle Paul said in 1 Timothy 4:1-2 that the era would be when "some will be withdrawing from the faith, giving heed to deceiving spirits and the teachings of demons, in the hypocrisy of false expressions." That

"Hey! I believe in salvation by will power!"

era is now. The doctrine of free will is perhaps the most clever and destructive of all these teachings. The main characteristic of a demonic teaching, according to the apostle Paul, is "the hypocrisy of false expression." When you detect hypocrisy and it's packaged in a false expression, then the source is demonic.

One of the most popular statements in the Christian religion today is, "Jesus saves." By itself, this statement is true. As presented by the Christian religion, however, it is hypocrisy packaged in a false expression. If Jesus saves, then why is salvation presented as a challenge? Why is it put forth as the result of a wise decision? Why do ministers at altar calls tell people to come down and "get saved?" Why is the exercise of the human will advertised as the all-important thing? What, exactly, saves? Is it Jesus or will power? I think this is an important question. Christianity believes it's will power. I know Christianity will not come out and say that; it can't afford to be that honest. Not one Christian person I know will say: *The key to my salvation was willpower. By the power of my will, I saved myself.* (But they should say it. It's the non-euphemistic way of saying, "I exercised my free will, and that's what got me in.") Instead, the wolf is given sheep's clothing. The wolf says: "I saved myself by exercising my will." But this is way too honest of a presentation. A plastic, public-relations-friendly sheep mask must be placed in front of the wolf. The sheep mask says: "Jesus saves." Ah, that's better. But does Jesus really save? If He does, then what is that big hairy thing behind the sheep mask threatening me with eternal death if I don't believe?

He did, but He didn't

What follows is a stunning example of free will hypocrisy in action.

I picked up a tract at my local grocery store called *Salvation Plain and Simple*, written by Dr. Curtis Hutson and copyrighted by Sword of the Lord Publishers. (I am one who now believes that grocery stores should stick to selling things like bread, milk and eggs, and leave religious hypocrisy to trained professionals.) Concerning the removal of sin—a key element of salvation—Dr. Hutson writes on pages 12 and 13 (emphasis mine):

> In order for an infinitely holy God to forgive the sinner, someone had to pay the debt. Someone had to bear the burden. That is where Jesus comes in. The Bible teaches that God took <u>every sin we ever have committed and ever will commit</u>, and laid those sins on Christ two thousand years ago at Calvary. Isaiah 53:6 says, "The Lord hath laid on him the iniquity of us all." <u>Every sin we have ever committed or ever will commit if we live to be a thousand years old</u>, God placed on Christ. The Bible says in 1 Peter 2:24, "Who his own self bare our sins in his own body on the tree..." 1 Peter

3:18 says, "For Christ also hath once suffered for sins, the just for the unjust, that he might bring us to God..."

The greatest truth that ever coursed through my brain is the truth of the substitutionary death of Jesus, that Jesus Christ actually took <u>all my sins, past, present, and future</u>, and bore them in His own body.

Friend, God looked down through the telescope of time and saw <u>every sin you would ever commit</u>. Then He put those sins in one big package and laid them on Christ, "The Lord hath laid on him the iniquity of us all."

I have underlined Dr. Hutson's most zealous and far-reaching comments concerning sin. These comments, by themselves, are accurate. Anyone reading them would thrill to hear of the completeness of Christ's victory over sin. But Dr. Hutson contradicts all of this nine pages later. His about-face occurs on page 21. I quote:

The worst sin in the world is not trusting Jesus Christ as Savior, and that is the only sin for which a man will go to hell.

Unquote.

DON'T LAUGH.
THIS IS STANDARD
CHRISTIAN DOCTRINE.

With the doctrine of free will, Satan has accomplished the seemingly impossible; he has caused a learned man—a so-called expert in the Scriptures—to completely contradict himself within nine pages of a popular Christian tract, without even realizing it. Here are the highlights:

- ◆ **Page 12:** Jesus took away all my sins, every single one.
- ◆ **Page 21:** Jesus did not take away the one sin capable of damning me: unbelief.

It's not that Dr. Hutson is dumb, but that Satan is devious.

Whitewash: Trusting in trust

In Matthew 23:27-28, Jesus compares the scribes and Pharisees to "whitewashed sepulchers which outside, indeed, are appearing beautiful, yet inside they are crammed with the bones of the dead and all uncleanness. Thus you, also, outside, indeed, are appearing to men to be just, yet inside you are distended with hypocrisy and lawlessness."

The two portions I read from Dr. Hutson's tract demonstrate the placement and lure of whitewash. Satan lures seekers into this tract by quoting Scripture and employing extravagant terminology promising the removal of sin. Here, again, is the whitewash:

♦ "God took every sin we ever have committed and ever will commit and laid those sins on Christ."

♦ "Every sin we have ever committed or ever will commit if we live to be a thousand years old, God placed on Christ."

♦ "Jesus Christ actually took all my sins, past, present, and future, and bore them in His own body."

♦ "Friend, God looked down through the telescope of time and saw every sin you would ever commit. Then He put those sins in one big package and laid them on Christ."

This is the outside of the tomb. The words appear beautiful and just. And they are. But these are *only* words. They are only the words that conceal the substance of Satan's favorite message, a message designed to keep people from understanding the cross. That message is: *Jesus did not do it all. It is up to you to finish the work of salvation.*

Let me repeat: the above is the substance of Satan's favorite message. And the doctrine of free will accommodates it perfectly.

Because now we look inside the tomb. We probe beneath Satan's promises of a "well-message" (that is, of a "gospel"), to see what we find. What we find is uncleanness, hypocrisy, and lawlessness. We find the bones of dead doctrine. We find a disgusting pile of death. *We* must appropriate the attempt Christ made to save us. And so Christ is not the mighty Savior of whitewash advertising, but rather the weak end of a formula that requires our vital contribution.

We, as hopeful seekers, walk away shaking our heads. It all sounded so good; it looked so beautiful. But it was just another heap of bones, another challenge to overcome our own sinning selves. We must somehow summon the energy to become worthy of Christ's work. Alas, there is "still one sin which will send us to hell," and it is our own human inability, the same millstone that has plagued us from birth. The result? We perceive God now as a hypocrite. He has wonderful ideas, but He cannot follow through on them. We are turned from Christ to seek another religion; one that will not lie to us.

And Satan smiles.

Dear Christian Jesus

Just great. There is only one sin that will send me to hell—unbelief—and it's the only sin You didn't die for. You went through all that pain to die for greed, gluttony, prostitution, murder, adultery and pride, when none of these matter if in the end I have faith. You left heaven for Calvary because You wanted to save people. Not a great job, if you ask me; see how few believe. Your efficiency rating is terrible. All You had to do was die for the killer sin, leave the rest, and everybody gets saved. Instead, You leave the killer sin hanging, die for forty million non-essentials, and ninety percent of humanity goes to hell. Was the sin of human unbelief too hard? Was it beyond the reach of Your blood? Or did you leave salvation up to us so that we, not You, could get eternal glory?

Thank God That Jesus Isn't a Christian

My apology, reader. I wrote that bit on the previous page to make you see the folly of it. Jesus *did* die for all sin, including the sin of unbelief. And the cross is for the glory of God, not man. Salvation is God's accomplishment, not ours. The result of this is that even those who disbelieve now will eventually live with God for eternity, for God must justify all who became sinners through Adam (Romans 5:19), and become all in all (1 Corinthians 15:28). How will it happen? The same method by which it happened for you--or have you forgotten already? God will overcome human stubbornness and impart belief (Romans 12:3). *Simple*.

Another wall of whitewash

Yet another whitewashed wall rises from this tract, on page 16. This wall promises a total reliance on the work of Christ. It promises the elimination of any human effort toward God's plan of salvation. The wall is constructed this way:

If you try to add anything to what Jesus has done, no matter how good the addition may be, you are saying by your actions, "I am not really satisfied with the payment Jesus made." It is not the death of Jesus Christ on the cross plus my baptism that saves. It is Jesus alone...If I trust Jesus Christ ninety percent and something else ten percent, the ten percent destroys the ninety. The ten percent says I am not fully trusting Christ.

The whitewash is brilliant and pleasing. But now enter the tomb and see the bones. I have underlined them. They lie on page 17:

> To show that we are fully satisfied with the payment, we <u>must</u> cease to trust any and everything else and trust Jesus alone. I <u>must</u> cease to trust my good works, no matter how good they may be. I <u>must</u> cease to trust my church membership, no matter how good my church may be. I <u>must</u> cease to trust my baptism, no matter how beautiful the ordinance. I <u>must</u> cease to trust my good life, no matter how pure and noble.
>
> In order to show God that I am satisfied with the payment made, <u>I must trust Jesus Christ completely</u>.

Sepulchers are very dark and the bones are not immediately evident. One must take a light into the tomb to see how unclean it truly is there. What Dr. Hutson insists the seeker must do for salvation on page 17 opposes the very thing he promised he would not do on the previous page. He promised, with a stroke of whitewash, to rely solely on Jesus Christ for salvation, or, as he puts it, "Jesus alone." There can be no trust in anything else, he said.

Except for human trust, of course. That's right. Because now Satan insists that the seeker *must trust completely* in Jesus Christ. Stop the film. There. Did you see the magician's hands? By insisting that a person *must* trust in Jesus Christ "alone," Satan denies the aloneness of Christ's work. Why? Because the work of Christ fails apart from human trust. Thus, in *having* to trust "completely in Jesus," the seeker does *not* trust completely in Jesus, but rather in his or her ability to trust in Jesus.

Rewind the film and watch it again. You must slow the action to see it. You must bring a strong light to the tomb, for here is deception at its fittest. Watch. Did you see it? Watch it again. Rewind the tape. Watch again. Isolate each small moment of action. With the enabling of God's spirit, you will detect movement in the corner. The movement is so quiet and small; this is deception crafted by otherworldly intelligence. It requires more than human ability to discern it. It requires the armor of God, for only the armor of God will enable you to "stand up to the stratagems of the Adversary" (Ephesians 6:11). And what of those unable to withstand these stratagems? Mil-

ARE WE TRUSTING IN OUR TRUST?

lions of people today who think they are trusting completely in Jesus, are, in reality, trusting in themselves.

And Satan smiles.

The 99.99% Syndrome

I finally got a free will guy one time to admit that his salvation was not all of Jesus. It took me about eight tries in one evening to crack the guy. He just couldn't bring himself to say it at first; he couldn't bear to confront his own doctrine.

I ask free will people what percentage of the work is Christ's, and most of them answer, "100%." It's the standard answer, the holy answer. It's the right answer. But then I follow up with, "Then why isn't so-and-so saved?" and the person is stumped because they want to say, "Because I believed and so-and-so didn't," but they know I'll torture them with the 100%. I'll ask them how much they now want to chisel from Jesus' 100% and give to themselves.

This guy was no different. He gave the right answer and I strapped him to the table. He was convinced that he had saved himself by believing, so he finally admitted, "Okay! Okay! Jesus didn't do *all* of it! But He did do 99.99% of it." The guy was really beginning to dislike me. The last thing he wanted was to publicly (and that's the key word) carve a valuable piece of the glory for himself from the precious 100% he had given to Jesus. He reveled in the self-glory in his mind, but he didn't want anyone to know about it. (You should have seen the look on people's faces when he finally admitted, "Okay! Okay! Jesus didn't do *all* of it!") He wanted to keep talking the Christian talk, but I yanked off the sheep mask and showed everyone, including the guy, what was behind it. He was as stunned as anyone to hear what he had said. But he recovered quickly, shut down his mind again and, to this day, continues to embrace the standard Christian hypocrisy.

Everyone at the Bible study that evening—everyone except the guy—learned a lesson about whitewash. Even if Jesus does 99.99% of the work, it's still the .01% human contribution that saves. Put nine nines to the right of the decimal point—it doesn't matter. With the free will doctrine, .000000001% on the human side saves as well as seven fewer zeroes. More nines to the right of the decimal point is only more whitewash. No matter what the numbers, the Jesus side tries, but the human side saves. Why not just make it 1% Jesus and 99% us? It's the same result as before, it's just a lot uglier without the whitewash.

I drove home from that Bible study realizing this: the more nines one puts on the Calvary side of the equation, the harder Jesus tried, and the more monumental becomes the failure of Christ.

WHITEWASH 101:

According to the free will doctrine, the

99.99 9999 99% Jesus did

STILL DOESN'T SAVE.

It's the .00000 0001%

you **do that makes SALVATION happen.**

A really wrong parable

Christians liken salvation to God giving you a gift. "But it's just like any other gift," they say. "You have to accept it." This is the favorite Christian analogy for describing salvation. I've heard it a million times. It's their dearest pet. "When someone gives you a gift," Christians say, "you can either accept or reject it." I will admit that this is a suitable analogy for Christmas and

WISDOM FOR
BOYS & GIRLS

He wouldn't accept my gift, so I killed him.

Sunday School Lesson
5
GIFTS

Become imitators of God!
Ephesians 5:1

birthdays, but as a picture of salvation through Christ, it fails completely. It's all wrong. Here is an analogy of salvation through Christ:

Someone deposited a million dollars into your bank account two thousand years ago. For two thousand years, you have been wealthy. This is a fact concerning you. You may be struggling to pay your bills, or be wearing ratty clothes, or be wondering where your next meal is coming from, but none of these things alter the fact of your wealth. It is only when you are informed of this wealth that you can begin believing it, appreciating it, and using it. Because until you believe it, you can neither appreciate it nor use it. No one is asking you to believe in your wealth in order to make it true. You are being asked to believe *that* your wealth is true. It has been true for two thousand years. Now—will you believe it? Only then will you enter into a practical enjoyment of it.

The Army better than Christ?

It is near Independence Day as I write this, and I just saw a sign here at the Church of Christ in my town that well illustrates the error of Christian teaching concerning Christ. The sign says: "Freedom is not free. Christ died to free us from sin; the military sacrifices to free us from tyranny." Well, it seems to me that the military does a better job at its chosen field than Christ does at His.

Did the death of Christ free us from sin? Apparently not. If it did, then why do preachers say, "Come forward and be saved from sin." Does the sacrifice of the military free us from tyranny? Actually, yes. We go where we please, do what we want, worship what we will, all because of our military. Does one have to appropriate these benefits to make them true? No. Most of us were born into freedom; we did not have to decide on it. No one asked us to believe in freedom for it to be true. No one told us we had to come down to an altar to confess tyranny before we could enjoy freedom. Freedom was never an issue of belief, but of fact.

Someone might say, "But a person can leave the country and not accept the freedom from tyranny." This misses the point. In the military example, a person would have to do something extraordinary (leave the country), to escape the benefit. In the example of Christ, a person has to do something extraordinary (believe) to *earn* the benefit. One has to overcome ironclad, God-breathed hindrances to faith—hindrances such as "there is no one righteous, no not one" (Romans 3:10) and "not one is seeking out God" (Romans 3:11)—in order to become free from sin. Thus, the work of Christ as presented by the Christian religion is actually inferior to the work of the United States military. The military's work against

tyranny is a work of grace, while
against sin must be appropriated and
to be real. The military worked hard and
even for idiots who don't appreciate it. Ch
hard and struggled against sin, but it only w
those wise enough, holy enough, and righteous e
to believe it. Idiots go to hell.

USA.
GOD IS OUTGRACED;
IDIOTS ARE SAVED.

Hell, heaven and back

It is a rare Christian publication that lays its bones
outside the tomb, but I have one. It is an advertisement
for the Greentown Church of God of Greentown, Ohio.
The ad appeared in the Canton *Repository* on September 27, 1998. The ad is titled, "Extreme Relevance" and
begins like this:

the work of Christ
properly believed
won freedom,
ist worked
orks for
nough

some of which are
evant decision that
decision deals with
going to do about

on to announce
will determine
forward. But I believe the
honesty to be inadvertent, for the very next statement is
whitewash quickly applied:

> The Bible is a progressive account of how God meets
> humanity's greatest needs through His Son, Jesus.

Strange. I am transported from the hell of determining my own eternal destiny, to an able God Who, through His Son, has met my greatest need. But this confuses me. Which is it? Do I need to stop sinning long enough to make a righteous, life-altering decision, or has God met my greatest need and delivered me from the debility of sin and unbelief? The writer now applies another coat of his product, luring me farther away from a challenge to personal righteousness into what will surely bring me joy and peace:

God is the compassionate Judge Who provided a sufficient substitute to pay the debt you owe—He gave Himself. You are free! God has accomplished this through His Son, Jesus Christ, Who lived a perfect life.

At last, Someone has lived the perfect life. I certainly have not been able to do that. But God's own Son did do it. And the writer calls the work of this Son "sufficient." The word "sufficient" thrills me. The dictionary defines sufficient as, "adequate for the purpose; enough." Then the tract says: "You are free!" If I'm free, then I'm saved as well. Right? Well, no. Alas. I am not saved, and neither am I free. The word "sufficient," whose definition is "adequate" and "enough," has proven to be false advertising. The word "free" is false as well, never mind the exclamation point. Christ is not enough, I am not free, I am not saved, because the ministers of hypocrisy at the Greentown Church of God are not quite finished dispensing their tortures. These writers, who have jerked me from hell to heaven, are returning me to the grave. At the last, I am tugged by a bony hand into the tomb where it all began. All emphasis here is mine:

God is still offering all these things today—full pardon, full payment, and full entry into Heaven for eternity. In order to receive this incredible gift of eternal value, we <u>must</u> first of all repent of our sins and place our complete faith and trust in Jesus Christ alone for salvation. Then Jesus commands His followers to be baptized just as He was. Then the balance of our lives <u>must</u> be lived in loving, grateful obedience to Him.

Where have I seen that "must" before?

And now, finally, into the darkest depths of sepulcheric despair:

> But before you decide, remember that thousands of years from now, your eternal residence will still be determined <u>solely</u> by this extremely relevant decision about Jesus. We're here to help with that decision because God has entrusted His Church with the responsibility of telling every person on earth this wonderful news. In light of what's at stake, we're taking God at His Word. How about you?
>
> Signed,
>
> **Pastor Don A. Deremer**
> CrossView Christian Church
> **Pastor F. Dale Senseman**
> Greentown Church of God

How about me? Well, thanks for asking. I'm going to find a loaded gun and aim it at my head. I can't live the balance of my life in loving, grateful obedience to Christ. I can manage this once in a while, but things happen. My spirit is willing, but my flesh is weak. I wish I was more like you guys, but I'm not. Since you say I *must* live the right kind of life in order to be saved, then I guess I'm doomed to an eternity without God. If only Jesus saved sinners—*then* I'd be in. If only my salvation was determined solely by Jesus, rather than solely by my "extremely relevant decision about Jesus"—then I would be saved.

I guess I should at least thank Jesus for the offer. At least He tried. Thanks to you guys, too. Thank you, Pastors Deremer and Senseman, for the wonderful news. I'm so glad God has entrusted you with the responsibility of telling every person on earth this liberating message. I can't for the life of me see what possible comfort it offers, or what is so wonderful about having to live a righteous life or be tortured forever, but if you say it's wonderful, then I guess it is. After all, you are trained

"First they told me Jesus saved me, then they told me I had to save myself, then they told me Jesus saved me, then they told me..."

ministers and I am just a layperson. Thank you for being Christ's humble servants and for taking God at His Word. I wish everyone could do it so well.

It's unbefrickinlievable.
Christian Daily News
Vol. 17, Iss. 3 July 10, 2005

In Little Rock today, a helpless yet extremely clever infant decided of its own free will to be rescued from a burning building.

Firefighters, responding to the infant's sovereign decision, rushed into the building and "rescued" the child.

Never before in fire-fighting history has an unconscious child shown such unbendable resolve. The firefighters, able to do only what the infant believed they could do, were amazed at the marvelous physical feats this senseless weanling forced them to accomplish.

As the baby regained consciousness, it was asked by a *Christian Daily News* reporter to detail exactly what happened. While we are not able to confirm the quote, the reporter is fairly certain that the infant said, "Uggdaa-buhh-dee-goo."

Savior of the helpless

Helpless:(help'lis), *adj.* **1.**unable to help oneself; weak or dependent. **2.** deprived of strength or power; powerless; incapacitated.

According to so-called men of God today, God offers "helpless sinners" a "general invitation" to "accept" His Son. Did you catch the absurdity of expecting helpless people to do something? If so, then you're already far ahead of trained professionals. Keep moving.

Romans 3:11 says, "Not one is seeking out God." Is this the human's fault? No. Why? Because Romans 11:32 says, "God locks up all together in stubbornness." Why would God do that? The answer is in the second half of the same verse, Romans 11:32: So that He can "have mercy on all." Anyone can save someone halfway in the boat. God saves the helpless.

In the ninth chapter of Acts, an extremely stubborn and helpless-to-save-himself person named Saul of Tarsus is en route to Damascus to arrest and kill Christians. Before he could even say, "Praise the Lord," Saul was on the ground beholding Christ's glory. This was not a general invitation to fall off a horse. Saul (Paul) wrote later: "The grace of our Lord overwhelms" (1 Timothy 1:14). "Overwhelms" reminds me of Niagara

Falls. A person walking out from under the falls would not need to make a decision whether or not to get wet.

Paul became the rule of salvation, not the exception. He told Timothy he was "a pattern of those who are about to be believing on Him" (1 Timothy 1:16). This does not mean that everyone gets pitched off a pony and blinded. But the principle is the same: Salvation operates in spite of us, not because of us.

Some think we have to get unhelpless long enough to call upon God. It would be nice if we could, but Romans 3:11 says we can't: "Not one is seeking out God." We are so helpless, in fact, that God has to give us the very faith we need to seek Him. This is why Romans 12:3 says that God parts to each the measure of faith. Don't I believe in the free will of man? No. I believe in the free will of God.

Here is what the "general invitation" doctrine is saying: God pulls into your driveway and, finding your house burning down, honks the horn a couple times. Being a hands-off God, (the essential teaching of free will), He then closes His eyes, plugs His ears and starts humming loudly to Himself so that He will not be tempted to influence your decision to either get into or not get into His car. From this point on, it's entirely up to your strength and your wisdom to open the door and get in. Never mind that you're upstairs lying unconscious on the floor (see "helpless," Romans 5:6). And you better hurry, because this buggy's moving on. Once God pulls out of the driveway, your chance to get in the car is over. (As if God leaves Christ's work on Calvary to chance. But so we're told.) The really crazy part about this "general invitation" business is that those who believe it call it "salvation by grace." Hm. It sounds more to me like "salvation by being strong enough and smart enough to get into God's car

"Absolutely totally helpless invalid!
I'll give 'im ten more minutes."

while God is closing His eyes, plugging His ears and humming to Himself."

Romans 5:6, layman's terms

This is salvation by grace: God pulls into your driveway and, finding you nowhere in sight and your house burning down, lays His own neck on the line and runs up the stairway, through the flames, and into your bedroom. Finding you unconscious on the floor in your underwear, He picks you up, carries you out of the house, down the sidewalk and out to His car. At the car, He cradles your limp frame in His left arm while opening the door with His right hand. Then He straps you into the front seat next to Him, slams the door and starts off to glory. Once you come to, He does let you say "I believe! I believe! I confess Your name!" Due to His gracious nature, He also lets you check the rearview mirror for Him occasionally, run the power windows up and down and fool with the radio. This is called being a "fellow worker with God" (1 Corinthians 3:5-9).

Then what is belief?

If human belief cannot save, what is its purpose? Human belief is a gift of God that acquaints people with something God already did. Romans 12: 3 says that God parts to each a measure of faith. Philippians 1:29 says that God graciously grants people to believe. These two verses alone disprove free will. People do have faith and they do have wills, but the believing and the willing

WE ARE NOT SAVED BECAUSE
WE BELIEVE;
WE BELIEVE BECAUSE
WE ARE SAVED.

originated outside themselves. *Belief is a gift of God.* It is a gift that follows salvation; it does not precede it. We are not saved because we believe, we believe because we are saved. God gives belief to acquaint us with an already-accomplished work: "He has saved us." For "God *is* the Savior of all mankind, especially of believers" (1 Timothy 4:10). What we may believe today cannot save us, for salvation occurred two thousand years ago at Calvary. Faith says: "I believe what happened then." It does not say: "I believe what was *attempted* then, which only happens now." That is the subtle lie. But no. Salvation is the deposit in your account that makes you rich. Belief is the gift that acquaints you with your wealth. It is, as 1 Timothy 2:4 states so precisely, a "coming into a realization of the truth."

Absolute truth vs. relative truth

Then why does Paul say to the Philippian jailer in Acts 16:31, "Believe on the Lord Jesus, and you shall be saved"? Paul is responding to the jailer's question, "What must I be doing that I may be saved?"

Turn to Ephesians 2:8-9. At first glance, these two verses appear to contradict Acts 16:31. "For in grace, through faith, are you saved, and this is not out of you; it is God's approach present, not of works, lest anyone should be boasting." Note this: In grace, *you are saved.*

It's a done deal. Christ saved you two thousand years ago. He did the same for the Philippian jailer. Christ's work procured salvation for you, and you, and you. You may or may not believe it yet, but it doesn't change the fact.

The faith of the context is Christ's, not yours. "And this is not out of you." What is not out of you? The faith. Galatians 2:16 says that we are "justified by the faith of Christ." His faith buys salvation, and the personal faith given you causes you to realize it. The personal faith given you brings you "into a realization of the truth" (1 Timothy 2:4). Of what truth? The truth that He saved you two thousand years ago.

Then what is the Philippian jailer asking? Consider this: Which aspect of salvation are we considering in this context? Are we considering the salvation that was won for this jailer at Calvary, or his realization of that salvation? Answer: his realization of it. I can prove this from the Greek, if you can stand it.

There are five different forms of the Greek verb: 1) incomplete, 2) indefinite, 3) complete, 4) indefinite-complete, and 5) middle. The Concordant Literal New Testament indicates these forms by superlinear markings next to the verbs. I want to focus now on the incomplete and the complete forms.

An incomplete verb form indicates ongoing action. This is expressed by adding *am, is,* or *are* to the verb and the ending *-ing*. Example: "I am sweating over this Greek grammar lesson." With the incomplete verb form, we don't know if you sweated yesterday, or if you're going to sweat tomorrow; we only know that you are sweating now, and are continuing to sweat. The complete verb form, on the other hand, gives the state resulting from an action. It is prefixed by *have, has,* or *had.* The complete verb form of our example would be: "I have sweated over this Greek grammar lesson." The complete verb form is a done deal. It is something that happened in the past.

Now watch this. In Acts 16:31, the verb form is incomplete. This is clearly indicated in the Greek. This jailer is saying, in effect, "What must I be doing that I may be being saved?" He's not talking about the salvation that was a done deal at Calvary, but his present experience. In Ephesians 2:8-9, however, the verb form is complete. Here, we *are* considering the done deal at Calvary. In the Greek it would be: "For in grace, through faith, you are ones having been saved."

In fact, here's the way it looks in my Concordant Greek Text:

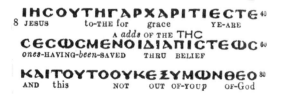

And here's the passage from Acts 16:31:

ΚΥΡΙΟΙΤΙΜΕΔΕΙΠΟΙΕΙΝΙ 60
masters   ANY ME   IS-BINDING TO-BE-DOING THAT

ΝΑCΩΘΩΟΙΔΕΕΙΠΑΝΠΙCΤΕ 80
31   I-MAY-BE-BEING-SAVED.THE YET THEY-say BELIEVE!

ΥCΟΝΕΠΙΤΟΝΚΥΡΙΟΝΙΗCΟ 200
     ΟΝ   THE   Master   JESUS

ΥΝΚΑΙCΩΘΗCΗCΥΚΑΙΟΟΙΚ 20
   AND   YOU-WILL-BE-BEING-SAVED YOU AND THE HOME

Many years after the end of World War II, a handful of Japanese soldiers on isolated islands in the South Pacific still believed the war was on. This is true. Being cut off from radio, television and newspapers, these men continued a watchful defense of their islands, albeit against a nonexistent enemy.

Now imagine that you are an evangelist visiting a group of these men on one of these islands. Your evangel is: "Gentlemen, the war is over." This is your good news. It is the equivalent of Paul speaking the word of the Lord to the Philippian jailer (Acts 16:32). Paul probably told the jailer: "Christ died for your sins" (1 Corinthians 15:3). Its spiritual counterpart is found in Ephesians 2:8-9: "In grace, through faith, are you saved." Paul would not have taunted the Philippian jailer with something that could be true only if the price was right, that is, if his faith was sufficient. He told him what Christ had accomplished for him on the cross. The Philippian jailer, naturally, wanted to know how he could be experiencing and enjoying this marvelous salvation; he wanted to know how he could be *being* saved, that is, how this salvation, which was an historical fact, could be becoming part of his present experience. "Simply by believing what I'm telling you," said Paul. "Simply by believing that it's true."

Now, would you have told the poor Japanese soldiers that the cease fire—an historical fact—was true only if they believed it was true? If you were a standard-issue Christian evangelist, you might. Such an idiotic message as "World War II is over only if you believe it's over" parallels the modern Christian message of "Christ saved you two thousand years ago only if you believe He did." But if you actually understood the message you were presenting, you would tell the soldiers: "This cease fire I'm reporting to you is a done deal; the war is over, fellows. You can believe it and start enjoying life again, or you can not believe it and keep fighting your imaginary war. But whether you believe it or not, the war is over, and it has been for some time now."

Do you see how this cease-fire evangel parallels the evangel of Ephesians 2:8-9? Do you see how it accords with the complete verb form? With a done deal? Do you see how it contradicts the Christian message? Whenever scripture speaks of the human doing something to be saved (as in Acts 16:31), God inspired the writer to use the incomplete verb form, indicating relative truth. Whenever scripture speaks of what Jesus Christ did for all (we're speaking of absolute truth now, as in Ephesians 2:8-9), God inspired the writer to use the complete verb form. Isn't that great? God is a genius.

Back to the enlightened soldiers. Compare their probable response to a proper presentation of your evangel with the incomplete verb form of Acts 16:31: "What must we be doing that this war may be being over for *us?*" And you say: "Believe what I tell you, and it will be being over for you."

Welcome to true evangelism.

"We told them that the war was over only if they believed it was over. So they shot Harry."

"God will not force Himself upon anyone."

When answering a question concerning salvation in a *Focus on the Family* magazine, Dr. James Dobson wrote: "God will not force Himself on anyone." (*Focus on the Family*, December, 1994.)

A distraught father had written Dr. Dobson concerning his teenage daughter. The girl was rebelling against her parents. Caught up with a fast crowd, she was mired in sin. The father had cried, pleaded, and prayed. Now he wrote, *Is there hope? Dr. Dobson, is there hope for my daughter?*

Dr. Dobson's answer, capsulated, was: *It is up to her, my friend. If she accepts Christ, there is hope. If she does not, well, God will not force Himself on anyone.* I remember this exact quote: "God will not force Himself on anyone." It was a thing I had heard many times before. How I hated it.

I am sorry, earnest seeker, but unless your daughter comes to her senses, she is lost. If this is to be, then your tears will mean nothing, for not even the perfect blood of Jesus Christ can save little girls who either do not know how or refuse to accept Him. Your precious daughter, I regret to say, is inches from eternal torment. The soft, golden hair you once stroked may be minutes from an eternity in the claws of Satan. I know that sounds harsh, but I must not shrink from telling it to you, for I am a minister of the Good News. From what you have told me, your daughter's salvation is quite doubtful. Again, I am sorry. Your daughter, of all people, needs God's blessed force. But God will not force Himself on anyone. He's a polite, eavesdropping God, a hopeful spectator in His own universe. He waits in the wings to see if any of humanity will like Him. He leaves these important decisions to us, my friend. I, myself, was wise enough to choose Him. Your daughter, apparently, is not.

Is your daughter sorry enough for her sin? Personally, I do not believe that she is. But for her sake, and for yours, I do hope things change. And soon. Good luck.

The amazing Dr. Dobson

How was Dr. James Dobson saved? His theology suggests that he made the truly wise and remarkable decision to seek out and appropriate God's salvation for himself. This *is* remarkable, for in doing this, Dr. Dobson has defied two universal laws, namely, 1) "Not one is seeking out God"—Romans 3:11, and 2) "There is no one righteous, no not one"—Romans 3:10.

Wake up, Doctor Dobson! You did not choose God, He chose you. Someday you will realize this; what a day it will be. Had God not forced Himself upon you, you would be like the rest of us infirm people—like that man's daughter, for instance—whom you now believe to be too foolish or too stubborn to know what's good for them.

"For Christ, while we are still infirm, still in accord with the era, for the sake of the irreverent, died. Yet God is commending this love of His to us, seeing that, *while we are still sinners*, Christ died for our sakes" (Romans 5:6,8).

Infirm people are helpless, Dr. Dobson. Sinners cannot save themselves. Someday you will realize how infirm you really were. Again, what a day that will be.

Thank God that the Son of His love forced Himself into our precious, self-sufficient lives to save us from ourselves. Jesus saved us while we were yet infirm, yet irreverent, yet in accord with the era. He died for our sakes. He forced Himself into our well-walled worlds, crumbling the confines of our crippled hearts.

He sent His Son, Who emptied Himself of His celestial glory to hang broken, bleeding, and separated from His Father on a cursed tree—for our sakes. We watched Him there. We saw Him look upon those who had stripped Him of His last human garments and nailed Him to the cross. His eyes moved among them, from the height of the cross, first to one, then to another. His eyes possessed a tender fluidity, an unearthly love that was not of men. Then, with anguished breath, through

a tongue swelled from thirst, He said, "Father, forgive them…"

Our knees trembled when He said that. *Why* did He say that? *How* could He say it? Had He *really* said it? We knew then that we were no better than the Roman soldiers, no better than the Jewish priests who delivered Him to death. His words undid us. We had been content to live our own lives, to go our own way, to seek scenes for our life that were easily more joyous, more blessed, more personally satisfying than this bloody hill. But then, we looked at Him.

Something about Him drew us. It was the Father, for none can come to Christ unless the Father draws them (John 6:44). And when we looked at Him, He returned our gaze with those same eyes, fluid and celestial.

"God, *no!*" we cried, and it just came out of our mouths; we could not help saying it; we could not take it back; we had betrayed our weakness. Then we fell with an abandon foreign to us to the dust beneath the cross, holding our wet faces behind our fingers, weeping uncontrollable tears at the foot of the wood. We could not have done that apart from the force of the cross. The cross was of God, and God was the cause of our falling tears.

And thus did God, through His Son, force Himself upon us. He had done something so deep, so wonderful, so unlike anything we would have done, that, given tens of thousands of years, none of us would ever have dreamed it, let alone accomplished it, let alone applied its accomplishment to our enemies.

He reached and rescued us. He pressed through the veil of our stubbornness and rescued us from ourselves. Thank God that He did. Without Him, what would we have? Apart from Him, what would we do? We need Him every moment of every day. We cannot afford an instant of self-sufficiency. What an ash heap of human pride is the saying: "God will not force Himself on anyone." That is the lie of Satan. Yet how many who claim the name of Christ believe and teach it.

This prayer, then: Father, continue to force Yourself into our lives. If it was up to us, we would not have You. We do not know what is good for us. We, like the humbled Job, cannot arrange our case because of darkness (Job 37:19). And as Jeremiah said under inspiration of holy spirit: "The way of a man is not in himself, nor is it in a man who walks to direct his steps" (Jeremiah 10:23). Continue to overrule and override our foolish desires and our foolish ideas about how things should be. We are nothing without You.

Cause us to lean not on our own understanding, or to imagine that we could have done anything good apart from Your force. *Cause* us, in all things, to give place to You as the One Who orders our steps (Proverbs 20:24).

Even the great apostle Paul said that You *make* us competent (Colossians 1:12). This is wisdom from above. Our competency cannot originate, continue or consummate within ourselves. All praise and honor and glory to You, Father, the Force of the universe.

Don't shoot the messenger

We now understand that God gives the belief and faith necessary for salvation. But this leads us to a startling and initially troubling conclusion: He has not given this belief and faith to others. While this may be a hard pill to swallow at first (I recommend a little orange juice), it is nonetheless true. But as I will show, this is not a problem. Truth is never a problem. Discarding error is the problem.

Matthew 13:11 records these words Jesus spoke to His disciples: "To you has it been given to know the secrets of the kingdom of the heavens, yet to those (the throng) it has not been given."

Hear Him again in Matthew 11:25- "Jesus said, 'I am acclaiming Thee, Father...for Thou hidest these things from the wise and intelligent.'"

What does the Master say of Jerusalem in Luke 19:42? "If you knew...what is for your peace! Yet now it was hid from your eyes."

Could it be that God purposely kept some from

believing His Son? You may be tempted to think that the "wise and intelligent" nailed their own coffins, or that Jerusalem got stubborn apart from God. Resist that temptation. I challenge you to read what these verses say, not what the "wise and intelligent" tell you they say. God is a causer, not a reactor. Consider the above in light of the following:

♦ Romans 11:8- "Even as it is written, God gives them (Israel) a spirit of stupor, eyes not to be observing, and ears not to be hearing, till this very day."

♦ Romans 11:32- "For God locks up all together in stubbornness."

♦ Romans 9:18- "Consequently, then, to whom He will, He is merciful, yet whom He will, He is hardening."

To the mind unprejudiced by traditional teaching, these verses say one thing: God is responsible for human unbelief. Don't shoot the messenger. This truth is probably causing yet another seemingly inescapable problem to trouble you. Allow me to place the problem squarely before you and offer a solution to it in the plainest possible language. I choose English.

God-inspired stubbornness

If you believe in either the annihilation or eternal torment of unbelievers (unbelievers such as your Uncle Horace, for instance) then you have encountered a serious problem. I have just shown from the Scriptures that God is responsible, not only for withholding Himself from Uncle Horace, but also for locking up Horace in stubbornness. Now look around you. The world is an oblate spheroid from the weight of people like your Uncle Horace; the spiritually stubborn account for most of humanity. My question to you is: what happens to these people when they die in this condition? You say that everyone gets an opportunity to believe, in this life, before God sends them to hell for eternity. Hm. Let's test this theory. Consider Israel.

In Romans 11:8, Paul writes that, even as it is written, "God gives Israel a spirit of stupor...till this very day." Paul was quoting Isaiah 29:10. Israel's divinely-inspired stubbornness, then, dates at least to Isaiah's time. (See also Isaiah 63:17 and 64:7-8.) Paul wrote Romans around the summer of 58 A.D. Isaiah lived around 750 B.C. Here alone are approximately 800 years of God-inspired stubbornness. And what of the nearly 2000 years of stupor since? A lot of Jews have died unbelievers in 2800 years. And God, Who has not only made them stubborn (Romans 11:8, 11:32) but also holds the keys of death (Revelation 1:18), is responsible. Does your theology have an answer for this?

The "Oh well!" creed

Calvinists are people who belong to a religion invented by John Calvin. John Calvin did see the truth of the sovereignty of God. He acknowledged that members of Christ's body are predestined for it long before birth, and wholly apart from personal merit. That's easy enough to see; Ephesians 1:4-5 and Romans 8:29 prove predestination to be a fact. But what of the billions of people who aren't predestined for heaven? What about

MODERN DAY CALVINISTS

"Oh, well!"

the horrible problem of a God who purposely feeds hellfire with divinely-hardened flesh?

Calvin did have a problem with the thought of a sovereign God bringing billions of people into the world, only to send most of them to an eternity of torment. Did Calvin solve this problem? Yes, but in a weird way: he no longer considered it a problem! That's right. John Calvin finally threw up his hands and decided that this was okay with him. Today, therefore, one of the shortest creeds in Calvinism is: "Oh well!" This creed is repeated a great deal at the funerals of unbelievers. Calvinism, and the infamous "Oh well!" creed, so infuses the heart with Christian love that its founder once had a disagreeable Spanish theologian, Michael Servetus, burned at the stake in Geneva in 1553. This is no joke. I guess Mr. Calvin figured that Mr. Servetus was going to hell anyway, so he may as well get him accustomed to the heat.

Song and dance

At the other end of the spectrum stand the Arminians. These people followed a man named Jacobus Arminius, who rejected Calvin's predestination teaching of pure grace. Arminius believed that salvation was available to everyone, but only individuals who exercised their free wills could take hold of it. This is what most Christians today believe. Most Christians today are in fact Arminians. The Arminians had to ignore a load of scripture verses teaching the sovereignty of God. They swept so many sovereignty of God verses under their theological rug that this rug soon resembled a beret on the Matterhorn. But at least they relieved God of responsibility for sending people to hell; yes, the irresponsibility of God was *their* preferred doctrine. I'm sure God sent them a thank-you note for the marvelous public relations work they accomplished on His behalf.

"If you go to hell, it's your own stupid fault!" is the Good News of the Arminians. This bogus gospel is passed down to the present day, whitewashed ("Jesus saves"), and preached as truth in almost every Christian church in America. It even makes some people in these churches want to wear fancy robes. But the doctrine, "if you go to hell, it's your fault!" has a sinister side effect (as if the doctrine isn't sinister enough) that not many pause to consider. That side effect is: "If you go to heaven, it's ultimately to your credit." This deduction is unavoidable, though rarely thought about and even less frequently spoken. But if going to hell is one's fault, how can staying out of it be anything but one's credit? If I can be stubborn enough to lose my salvation—or never gain it in the first place—it is self-evident that I can be savvy enough to obtain and keep it. And indeed, according to Arminian types, I better be. This is the reason most Christians can't help sticking their noses up in the air, at least a little bit. This little song and dance of blaming others without crediting oneself is known in scripture and elsewhere as hypocrisy. The concept of salvation by human effort is known as salvation by works. In the camps of Christendom, these things are never called what they truly are. The things are whitewashed there, dressed like sheep, and presented to the masses with a humble-sounding, "Praise the Lord."

Want to get persecuted? Walk into your average evangelical Christian church today and suggest to them that the blood of Christ was shed for—and will ultimately save—everyone. For some reason, this news will stab their hearts, infuriate them, and make them hate you

MODERN DAY ARMINIAN

"I don't know why people just don't choose Christ...like *I* did!"

with a pure, evangelical fury. Of course, they'll white-wash that, too; they have buckets and buckets of the stuff. Since they can't crucify people today, they will merely persecute you socially and ask you to leave. This righteous antagonism is usually carried out by the worship team.

Want to hear some sense?

I will now solve all the above difficulties and relieve your troubled mind.

The problem, restated, is: 1) No one can believe in God unless He gives them belief, 2) He refuses to give belief in this lifetime to most of humanity, hardening their hearts to boot, and—here comes the problem—3) He allegedly sends those whom He has hardened (without the proper clothing, one would assume) to an eternity of hellfire.

You will notice that the Calvinist and the Arminian viewpoint have one common point: a belief in eternal torment. This is the falsehood that derails both trains. The Arminians duck the horror of the orthodox hell by making God not liable for sending folks there. The ticket out? Free will. Free will is one of the easiest heresies to disprove, but it doesn't matter. Arminian-types who believe in eternal torment are in the embarrassing position of having to stare sovereignty-of-God verses in the face and deny them. I've witnessed the phenomenon. But at least, unlike Calvinists, they resist a God who damns people on purpose. Calvinists, delicate souls, simply recite the "Oh well!" creed and go home.

If one takes what is correct about Calvinism and correct about Arminianism, then discards the common error between them, one arrives at truth. The Calvinists are correct in that only God can give people belief; they are wrong in assuming that God has predestined only a select group from humanity for eternal life. The Arminians, on the other hand, are correct in that salvation is for all; they are wrong in teaching that it is up to man to appropriate this salvation. Put the two truths together and we discover that salvation is, indeed, for all, and God will eventually give all belief.

Simple, really.

The doctrine of eternal torment is gross error and a twisting of God's revelation. I hope the suggestion that it even might be that makes you glad, rather than sad. If your heart is supple and your creed is susceptible to truth, then read on. Free will is an error that seeks to cover the error of eternal torment. It is a bad check written to cover a bad check. If a builder sets a crooked foundation, he must build the house askance to accommodate it. If he is an approved workman, however, he will destroy the faulty foundation and work harder to lay it aright.

VERSES THAT DISPROVE HUMAN FREE WILL

2 Corinthians 5:18- "All is of God."

Romans 11:36- "Out of Him and through Him and for Him is all."

Acts 17:25- "He Himself gives to all life and breath and all."

Daniel 4:35- "According to His will is He doing in the army of the heavens and with those abiding on the earth."

Ephesians 1:11- "God is operating all in accord with the counsel of His will."

OR THIS:

"It is not that you have chosen me; but it is I who have chosen you."

— *Jesus Christ, John 15:16*

Jesus must not be a Christian. Why didn't anyone tell Him it's the other way around?

Imagine

Imagine for a moment that eternal torment might be wrong. Imagine it to be the sorry result of one or two key scriptural words mistranslated. Imagine, if you can, that Jesus Christ really did remove sin, just as John the Baptist said He would (John 1:29). Imagine, too, that He will destroy the works of the devil, which Scripture says He came to do (1 John 3:8). Imagine, if you can, that He Who wills all to be saved (1 Timothy 2:4), is able to accomplish what He wills (Ephesians 1:11). Imagine that the same all dying in Adam will one day be vivified in Christ (1 Corinthians 15:22). In other words, imagine that the Second Adam will do greater good than the first did harm (Romans 5:18-19); this should not be hard to conceive. Imagine that He is the Savior of all mankind (1 Timothy 4:10), Who will abolish all death, including the second (1 Corinthians 15:26). And can you envision a universe finally freed from sin, all creatures of all time ultimately reconciled to Him (Colossians 1:16-20)? Then rejoice, for you are on hallowed ground.

REJOICE.

God on Plan A

But before He can save all, God must lose all first. This is absolutely necessary. And so, "He locks all together in stubbornness, that He might have mercy on all" (Romans 11:32). Thus, the "fall" of humanity in the garden did not take God by surprise. How could anything take God by surprise? God did not resort—following the events of Eden—to Plan B. I am happy to tell you that God is still on Plan A, and the so-called fall was part of that plan. God has a plan (Ephesians 3:11). Imagine that.

Influence & Circumstance

The damning word in the phrase "free will" is not the word "will," but the word "free." According to the dictionary, to be free is to be "independent; exempt from influence." Can anyone be independent of God? I hope you would answer "no." We exercise our wills thousands of times daily, but none of us do it freely. Every decision and thought of humanity is the result of influence and circumstance, and God is the Author of all influence and circumstance.

The sovereignty of God

God needs a cross to reveal His salvation. He needs rotten Romans who know how to hammer people. He needs a foul priesthood to offer the Sacrifice. He needs, yes, a Judas Iscariot to deliver the Lamb. He needs enemies and sinners and whips and nails and vinegar and reeds to fulfill His Scriptures. And so, He gives Israel a spirit of stupor (Romans 11:8). He makes vessels of dishonor, to make His powerful doings known (Romans 9:21-22). He has made the wicked for this day of evil (Proverbs 16:4), and has created the ruiner to harm [His Son] (Isaiah 54:16). The mob in Jerusalem believe they have untrammeled wills, but they are doing precisely what He has designated beforehand to occur (Acts 4:27-28). None of them know that (1 Corinthians 2:8), but it doesn't matter. This was a scene choreographed by God (Ephesians 1:11), for our benefit (Romans 5:9). Good and evil are servants in His hand (Job 2:10).

The potency of the cross

And now, Jesus is on the cross. There is black here, and pain, and sin, and evil. Though we all recoil at it, this is a perfect backdrop for a revelation of grace. In fact, it is the only backdrop possible.

First Jesus says: "Forgive them Father, they know not what they do" (Luke 23:34). These words would not stun us apart from the setting of Calvary. Now comes an act: Jesus takes on Sin. The sky turns black; God turns His face; the universe pivots; a few of the people watching this drama return home in tears. Celestial powers are shaken and stupefied. This Christ is stripping off sovereignties and authorities, with boldness making a show of them, triumphing over them (Colossians 2:15), alone.

There is a veil in the temple keeping people from God. When Christ gives His spirit back to His Father and dies, this veil is torn clear through. No man could have done this because the veil was too heavy. God did this amazing thing to the veil. Since this time forward, no roadblock in heaven or on earth can keep God away. God is now conciliated to all mankind (2 Corinthians 5:19). This blessing has come to us through the blood of Christ's cross (Colossians 1:20). God no longer holds men's offenses against them (2 Corinthians 5:19). This same blood will reconcile all to Himself, both that in the heavens and that on earth (Colossians 1:20).

The cross saves everyone, but not all at once (1 Corinthians 15:22-23). Jesus Christ is a ransom for all, but the testimony of it will not be seen until the eras designated to show it (1 Timothy 2:6). God will one day be all and in all (1 Corinthians 15:28). How can

He be that if billions of the all remain dead or tortured?

Paul speaks of a time called the consummation, when death is to be abolished (1 Corinthians 15:26, 2 Timothy 1:10). If there will one day be no more death, then the time is coming when even the second death will cease to be. At this time, those formerly captured by it will be delivered into the life won for them by Christ on the cross. With no more death, nothing remains but life. Some come to Christ sooner, some come later. But eventually, all come.

THE MYSTERY CARD   by Martin Zender

"If the specter of logic or preponderance of scriptural evidence ever threatens your preconceived orthodox belief system again, Suzy, just say, 'Well, I guess it's just a *mystery!*'"

Free will or divine omniscience?

You can't have it both ways

Some people will warp predestination verses such as Ephesians 1:4 ("He chooses us in Him before the foundation of the world") and Romans 8:29 ("Whom He foreknew, He designates beforehand") in order to preserve their belief in human free will. They'll say: "God looks ahead of time to see what you're going to do, then comes back to His time and predestines you." This extravagant, unscriptural time game illustrates the desperation of the free will camp. That's not the worst of it.

If God has to look ahead of time to see what we're going to do, then God doesn't know everything. If He knew everything, He would not need to look ahead. Whoever believes in human free will believes in divine ignorance by default. Here's how that works: 1 John 3:20 says: "God knows everything." If God knows everything, then He knows ahead of time what's going to happen. And if He knows ahead of time what's going to happen, then whatever happens *has* to happen; it can't *not* happen. And if whatever happens can't *not* happen, then human free will—which assumes that eight billion people can either do or not do whatever they want—is pure illusion.

ISAIAH 46:10- "GOD TELLS THE END *FROM THE BEGINNING*"
-- not because He looks ahead to the end

"Well I'll be. Looks like I'm going to have to predestinate Bill."

The "especially" salvation

God is the Savior of all mankind, especially of believers (1 Timothy 4:10). He is not the Savior of all mankind, *exclusively* of believers. That would be the lie of the Christian religion. This verse alone proves that God will save all.

Note this: I am not a Universalist, so please do not call me that. People who belong to the Universalist cult disregard scripture and belittle the blood of Christ; they think God saves just because He's *nice*. I have nothing to do with either Universalists or Unitarians, and am capable of splashing hot coffee upon anyone calling me these sordid names. I am a believer in scripture, correctly translated. I am an advocate of the power of the cross and the ability of Christ to save humanity from all sin. God is love *and* He is righteous, and both these attributes met at the cross; this is what I'm about.

The word "especially," in 1 Timothy 4:10, is a very big word.

The "especially" there means that those who believe now do receive more. It is true that there are only a certain number of people chosen by God to believe in this life. I have established clearly in this book that only God can give faith, and that if God does not give it, faith does not come. I cannot, therefore, blame any person alive or dead for not having faith. Sometimes I'd like to, but I can't. I can only thank God that I do have it. Because I know that, apart from Him giving it to me, I would never have it, ever.

The day I finally realized that salvation was not of me, was a big day. This was years after I had become a so-called Christian. In the old days, I would say my salvation was "not of me," but I never really believed that. I was brainwashed into saying it, but not believing it. The day God revealed it to me—what a revelation. What a day. I had been a Christian for years, but I'm speaking now of the day I became a believer. There really was no difference, I discovered, between my flesh, my mortality, my ability to seek God, and the flesh, mortality, and ability of unbelievers. I was in the same boat as everyone else. This is humbling, when you finally see it. It breaks you and you cry. Were it not for God's grace, I would have been a Hitler, or a Manson, or a Dobson. It was Paul who said, "I am what I am by the grace of God." People repeat that by rote; they don't mean it. I used to repeat it and not mean it, too.

The revelation of grace was scary because I suddenly realized how thankful I should be. I used to not be overcome by great swells of thankfulness. Well, I thought I was a little bit worthy of eternal life. And I was, in my mind. After all, I believed. When I realized that God chose me to believe, and that He gave me the very faith needed to call out to Him (and the greater faith that ensued), I realized how helpless I'd been. I realized that if God hadn't done all that, I'd still be an unbeliever. I became so thankful then, so desperately thankful. I became less condemning of those not yet chosen to believe. It was not their fault. I finally saw it. *My God, it was not their fault.* Conversely, it was no more my credit. God had to take me out of church to restore to me a clear-thinking head.

Thanks to God, I did have something more. There was an advantage, I discovered, to being given belief now. I would live and reign with Christ during coming ages (Revelation 22:5), while those without faith would neither live nor reign then (Revelation 20:5). They would instead be dead while I reigned. This was the "especially" salvation of 1 Timothy 4:10. God gives immortality to all, eventually (1 Corinthians 15:22-28), but He gives it to some early so they can live and reign with Him through oncoming ages. These, He "especially" saves.

I learned that there were two glorious ages ahead: the thousand-year kingdom (Revelation 20:4) and the new heavens and new earth (Revelation 21:1). I learned that most people would be dead during these glorious times (Revelation 20:5). When I learned that this wasn't their fault, I felt sad for the people. But when I realized that they would eventually be given belief and live eternally with God, it mollified my grief. After all, what were two short eons compared with eternity? Nothing, relatively. Besides, as I said, the unbelievers would be dead. In the death state, there is no consciousness of time. This, also, was a surprising truth. I never knew it. It was always in scripture, but I was trained to ignore it. These people would not *know* they were dead. It was God's merciful provision. Jesus, in scripture, compared death to sleep (John 11:11-13). It comforted me that these people would be asleep and unaware that I was living and ruling with Christ. No need for me to feel guilty, then.

When one realizes that all is of God and that nothing, absolutely, is of oneself, one does stop condemning unbelievers. It does make one ask God, however: "Why

"Where will you spend eternity?"

This was the question posed on a church sign in my town. *Wrong question!* The answer, however, is that everyone will spend eternity in heaven with God and Christ. Why? Because sin is the only thing standing in people's way, and Jesus Christ took away the sin of the world at Calvary (John 1:29). Simple. What the sign meant to ask was: "WHERE WILL YOU SPEND THE EONS?" Not everyone will spend the eons with God and Christ. Only the chosen ones (referred to as saints) rule with Christ "for the eons of the eons" (this is the correct translation of Revelation 22:5.) No one knows who is chosen until the chosen ones jump up in response to a proper presentation of the gospel and say, "I believe!" The rest of mankind (the people who don't jump up) will be dead during the eon of the thousand-year kingdom (Revelation 20:5), as well as during the eon of the new heavens and new earth (Revelation 20:12-15). It's a bummer, yes, but certainly not the eternal disaster that Christianity makes it; when death is abolished, these people are granted immortality with Christ (1 Cor. 15:22-28).

WHERE WILL YOU SPEND THE EONS?

I exhort you today to believe the gospel: Christ Jesus died for your sins, was entombed, and rose from the dead three days later.

Jesus Christ saved you 2000 years ago.

How are you responding to that?

me and not them?" I did this. I wondered what it was. God simply said, "Because I chose you (Ephesians 1:4). Because I favor you. I chose you before you were born (Romans 8:29)." I said, "But don't you favor them?" God said, "I am the Savior of all mankind, *especially* of believers. I'm the Savior of them as well, and they will live with me forever. But it is simply not My plan for them to live during the coming two ages. They'll have no complaints because they'll be with Me forever. This comes about in its own eras (1 Timothy 2:5-6). For now, I'm working in a framework of time (Romans 16:26, the 'eonian God').

"Enjoy what I've done for you. Stop worrying about everyone else. No one would have any complaints if I consigned the entire human race to the second death. Who would complain about being asleep for two relatively short ages—unaware of the time—and then waking up to a life of eternal bliss? The miracle, Martin, is not that everyone will live with Me for eternity. The miracle is that I have chosen before the eons a blessed few who will rule and reign with Me during the coming two glorious ages of time (Revelation 22:5). That is the "especially" salvation of 1 Timothy 4:10. It delights Me

WHAT HAPPENS NOW TO THE
HUMAN PRIDE OF ACHIEVEMENT?

to do this. It's not that the rest are cheated, it's that you and the others I have chosen are especially blessed. You come into My life early, and are privileged. It is nothing of yourself (Ephesians 2:8-9). It is everything of My favor. You are privileged above and beyond the rest of humanity. This is in accord with the delight of My will (Ephesians 1:5), not your worthiness or accomplishment (2 Timothy 1:9). It delights Me to bring a select few in early. You are, as My Word says in Ephesians 1:12, 'Pre-expectant in the Christ.' So rejoice!"

"Okay!" I said. "Thanks!" And so I do.

In conclusion

If you begin an account of your salvation with the word "I," then you have something to boast about. The boasting may be Christianized (that is, hidden beneath layers of whitewash), but it's there. The gospel of Christ, however, eliminates all boasting. This is because it is an act of God, not man. After describing the nature of justification in Romans 3:21-26, the apostle Paul asks in verse 27: "What happens now to the human pride of achievement?" He answers his own question: "There is no more room for it."

Do you begin an account of your salvation with the word "God?" Good. You have repudiated the false teaching of human free will. You have rejected the false pride of human achievement. You have embraced the truth: salvation is of God and not of your decision concerning God. God has graciously granted you to be believing this. So rejoice.

"For who makes you different from anybody else, and what have you got that was not given to you? And if anything has been given to you, why boast of it as if you had achieved it yourself?" (1 Corinthians 4:7).

Got it? Good.
God bless you.
Martin

"A provocative, intellectual romp. You need to read this book!"
--Dwight Green
Ft. Worth Star-Telegram

martin zender

HOW TO
QUIT CHURCH
WITHOUT
QUITTING GOD

Why going to church today is unbiblical, un-Christlike, and spiritually risky.

COMING JULY 2012

FROM THE BACK COVER OF:

The First Idiot in Heaven:
Secrets of the Apostle Paul
(And why the meek merely inherit the Earth)

While on Earth, Jesus said some difficult things. He told the rich to give away all their money, and the joyful to become mourners. If you wanted to inherit the Earth, you had to be meek. If your eye offended you, no problem—as long as you plucked it out. A friend of mine said, "Can I start following Jesus on Monday? I'd like to enjoy the weekend."

Obviously, the words and commandments of Jesus are pure, perfect, holy—*and meant for Israelites.* Jesus Himself said, "I was not sent except to the lost sheep of the house of Israel" (Matthew 15:24).

Is it possible we have been struggling along someone else's path? What if the words in red were never meant to be our marching orders?

Several months after leaving Earth, the Jewish Messiah appeared as a very non-Jewish light to a self-righteous idiot en route to Damascus to kill Christians.

Up next? Not only a startling new destiny for believers (heaven instead of Earth) but a new message of pure grace for *all* humanity.

This is that story.

> ❝ Zender's genius lies in boiling complex theological concepts down to their essence. Never has Paul been plainer—or more fun to read. The apostle himself would have a hard time putting down this book. ❞

Dan Sheridan
The Zender/Sheridan Show
WBRI, Indianapolis

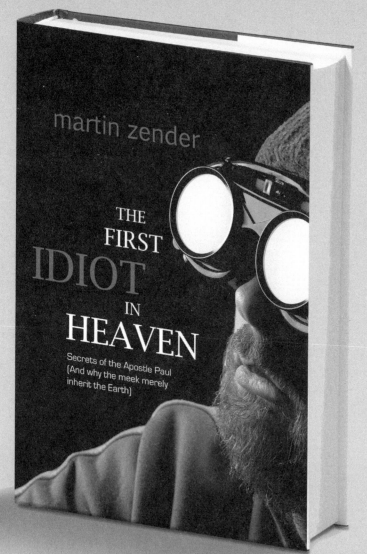

martin zender

THE FIRST IDIOT IN HEAVEN

Secrets of the Apostle Paul
(And why the meek merely
inherit the Earth)

According to Jesus, the meek inherit the Earth.
So what happens to the rest of us?

THE BEST NEWS YOU'VE NEVER HEARD. 30 ILLUSTRATIONS.

www.thefirstidiotinheaven.com